Ogehmawahbee,

Chippewa Warrior;

And His Incredible Journey During the Time of Relocation

A true story originally told in the oral tradition
by the Osogwin Story Tellers Mike Osogwin and John Osogwin
of the Chippewa (Ojibwa) People.

Retold by Mike Osogwin Jr. and Marianne Osogwin
Assisted by Moira Z. Wilson
Illustrated by Brian F. Wilson

All Text and Images © 2001. All Rights Reserved,
MZW Ink, Hessel, MI., USA.
First Edition
ISBN# 0-9708711-0-4

A Note to Parents.

Shortly following World War II, my father felt compelled to take me to see the actual confiscated films of the Third Reich. As we left the theater, I proudly turned to my father and said, "Daddy, I'm glad we're not like that!" My father's response in a soft sad voice, "We all are, don't ever forget it!" At fifty those words rang again in my ears as I heard the Osogwin tapes and heard this story told by both Mike Osogwin and his brother John Osogwin. Once more I was forced to recognize the "we" stood for man's inhumanity to man.

Because of the generosity of the co-author, Yvonne Peer and Editor, Susan M. Schacher, Lake Superior State University Press, the complete transcript of the taped story found in <u>Celebration of Indigenous Thought and Expression</u>, Susan M. Schacher, Ed. Sault Ste. Marie, MI: Lake Superior State University Press, Oral Tradition and Print: The Stories of Mike and John Osogwin, Moira Z. Dibert Wilson and Yvonne Peer, p. 163-172. published in 1996 has been included as an appendix to assist parents, students and educators.

In his excellent text, Charles E. Cleland states the case for Michigan Tribes in <u>Rites of Conquest: The History and Culture of Michigan's Native Americans</u>. Ann Arbor, MI: University of Michigan Press, 1993. Cleland states on page 198 and 199 the following concerning the times of relocation. "The story of the tactics used to separate Indians from their ancestral land holdings and their subsequent concentration on tiny reservations is perhaps the most morally despicable story in North American history. It is also one of the culturally most complex, involving a mix of paternalistic good will, racism, arrogance, and ignorance that is difficult to understand. Perhaps more important for today's world, these same events leave modern Americans with a legacy of guilt that powerfully influences the relationship between Indian and non-Indian citizens. ....Two national policies were eventually formulated as a means to promote American domination. The first was the removal policy during the first half of the century; this was later followed by the so-called civilization policy."

This story of the triumphal spirit of mankind contrasts against the dark background of the time of relocation. Mike Osogwin Jr., Marianne Osogwin, and I hope retelling this story helps to prevent future events of inhumanity no matter how small.
We dedicate it to our children and all other survivors.

Moira Z. Dibert Wilson

    Favorite often told stories always find a welcome ear. The room fell very quiet. Only the fire's crackle could be heard as the wind and snow curled about the home in Les Cheneaux, among the Islands near Mackinac on the shore of Lake Huron. Even though everyone knew the story, they wanted the story to warm their ears and hearts once more.

    Grandfather Michael-John spoke. "This story my Grandfather told me of my Great Uncle, Ogehmawahbee (o-geh-ma-wah-bee), brother of my Great Grandfather. Listen to the story of Ogehmawahbee, War Chief of the Bear clan. Ogehmawahbee loved his family and loved the Great Lakes so much that he braved all to return home to his people and to his family. His love and his strong vision kept him alive through a terrible time... the time of relocation. His story tells of the strength of one of the people in terrible times. His story is one of many.

"Ogehmawahbee lived with our people in the woodlands and islands of the Great Lakes. In summer, they traveled to Beaver Island way out on the clear blue waters of Lake Michigan. They speared and netted lake trout and sturgeon to feed our people. They dried fish for the coming harsh winter. They picked blueberries and strawberries from plants hung heavy with fruit. They grew squash, beans, and corn, the Three Sisters, to feed our people. But that summer, Ogehmawahbee's life and the life of the Chippewa People would change forever.

"You know that it was in the time of treaties. Michigan territory would soon become a state. Treaties were signed in Detroit and Chicago, but the Indians of the north didn't go to Detroit. They heard that a treaty boat would come to them with payment just as the English and French had brought payment before to the Indians of the north.

"One day as Ogehmawahbee stalked a deer in the woods near his village, he heard a cry arise from the far end of the village near the water's edge.

"'The soldier boats come! The treaty boats are coming!'"

"Now, even the bravest of men knows what fear is. He had heard stories at night around the fire of the big boats pushed by the winds that carried the United States soldiers to all the Indian nations of the Great Lakes. His dreams made him wary. In that moment, Ogehmawahbee felt afraid for his people.

"Would these U.S. soldiers come to make a peace treaty with the Chippewa? Would they bring payment as the French and British had? Once some of the Chippewa had joined other Anishnabeg to help the British. They had beaten the U.S. soldiers at Fort Mackinac. However, unfortunately, those voices around the fires said that the British had unfortunately returned the land that had been won following the War of 1812. As more and more settlers took the land, the Chippewa people had moved further north. Ogehmawahbee worried. He wanted peace, but soon there would be no place left for his people to live. The settlers just kept coming.

"All these things went through his mind as he ran to the beach to see the ships that he had heard so much about.

"Indeed, two ships had arrived at the village. The stories had all been true. The ships looked like tiny islands with great wings folding like gulls dropping to the water as they came to anchor in the stillness near the shore. Ogehmawahbee saw that each ship was much, much larger than any trader canoes that he had ever seen.
Black cloaks covered the name boards. Men scrambled on the rigging securing the sails. Soldiers stood silently on the broad wooden decks.

"A few soldiers and their leaders came ashore. They told of a feast to be prepared for the Indians. They spoke of gifts of cloth, blankets, pots and pans, and beautiful beads and jewelry. Tomorrow as many of the Chippewa as could come would be welcomed to the boats."

Michael-John paused and looked around the room. "You know, the soldiers knew what would attract the people into the boat. They knew that food, drink, trade goods, and cheap jewelry could trick the people.

"So the people gathered together to talk about the treaty ships that had come to them. Should they meet with the soldiers and talk of peace? Would there be war? Should they accept the soldiers' hospitality and gifts? In the end, after everyone had had a chance to speak, the elders would decide. That was how it had always been. The wise elders would know what was best to do.

"The elders decided that all the best warriors and women with grown children would go to the feast. They could receive treaty goods for those with tiny children and the old ones who could not easily go out to the ships. The warriors and the strong women would listen to what the soldiers had to say and then share it with the elders who would know what to do.

"The next morning, Ogehmawahbee prepared to go with the other warriors. His wife held their tiny daughter and watched him quietly. She said nothing, but he could tell that she had many thoughts. 'I will return, little one,' he said softly to his daughter as he touched her smooth cheek and looked into his wife's eyes. Then he turned and joined the others to go out to the ships.

"The warriors and the women climbed up the rope ladders which hung over the railings of the ships. On the decks the soldiers stood quietly at attention. Before the people, large hatches with great hinges stood open. In the hold of each ship, food and gifts covered great tables. Many of the warriors felt nervous to see the tables deep in the bowels of the boat. Why didn't the soldiers put the tables up on the deck in the sunshine? Wasn't there more room on the decks? But this was the treaty ship. What was there to fear? Besides... everything was all set up. Everything was ready for them.

"The soldiers coaxed the people down into the hull. 'Come see what we have brought for you,' they said. The people still didn't trust the soldiers. They were unsure just what to do. Surely, the soldiers felt friendly if they went to all this trouble. So, many of the people went below.

"Ogehmawahbee climbed down the stairs into the hull of the ship. Many different kinds of food, drinks, warm blankets, beautiful cloth, jewelry, beads, and iron pots and pans laid on the tables spread before him. A few of the people remained on the deck with the soldiers. The people and the soldiers exchanged greetings and gifts as was the custom.

"After awhile, the time came to return to their canoes and to share what they heard with the elders. The soldiers climbed the stairs first. Ogehmawahbee wondered why the people who were guests did not leave first. Wasn't it the polite thing to do?

"The soldiers' leader stood at the top step and spoke. He said 'The soldiers wanted to give the Indians a special farewell'.

"Suddenly, a shout arose from up on the deck. The sound of splashing water filled Ogehmawahbee's ears. What was wrong? He leapt to his feet... too late. A loud crash sounded above him as the hatches slammed shut. Heavy hinges and locks slid tightly into place.

"Those below were captured. Through the hatch grating, Ogehmawahbee could see the soldiers handcuff those who remained on deck. He heard the laughing soldiers throw some of the Indians overboard. The soldiers figured the shore was too distant. Shots soon rang out. Even in fear, Ogehmawahbee could smile as the soldiers fired at those who swam to shore. For Ogehmawahbee knew that, unlike the soldiers, the Chippewa were great swimmers. At least a few of the best warriors would get to shore to protect the village and to help the elders, the old ones, the women, and the children to safety. For this he gave thanks. He could hear the sails unfurl and the wind fill the canvas. His eyes sought the sun to sense the direction that they would take. He must remember.

"He must remember.

"The great ships sailed away into the big lake toward the place that we now call Chicago... taking with it the best warriors and the strong women of the Chippewa Nation.

"Now while all this was happening to Ogehmawahbee, the village learned what had happened. A great and terrible cry arose from the Chippewa people filled with sadness and anger. They mourned those whom they had lost... the strong protectors, the hunters, the providers... those who gave care, those who fed and clothed the people. They feared that they would never see them again. The cry rose on the wind as the people with one great voice prayed to the Creator for the safety and the lives of those taken in the ships. What a terrible loss this was. How could the old men and women, the young women, the children survive?

"They quickly packed what few belongings were necessary and fled their island home... leaving much behind. The people from Beaver Island traveled fast by canoe through the Straits of Mackinac, past Les Cheneaux, by the mouth of the St. Mary's River, near Drummond and Cockburn Islands and South to British Canada. They landed at a place called Manitoulin Island, or the Spirit Island as it is called in our language. They lived there with the other Chippewa who had escaped during the relocation time. The people built new longhouses and raised the children. Ogehmawahbee's wife and daughter would wait... no matter how long... for his return.

"Meanwhile those people who were captured traveled two days and two nights before the treaty ship landed in Chicago. In the port, the warriors were bound like animals, ropes around their necks tied to the neck behind. The soldiers knew that the Chippewa could run like deer, so they bound their wrists and ankles with rope. Now the people could not fight. They could not escape. They were empty handed. They had no weapons. They could not do anything.

"Empty filthy cattle cars stood waiting for the people. The cattle had long since been slaughtered and marketed. But on this day, no one loaded cattle for market. This day Indians were loaded into these cars.

"From many nations, the people came bound and helpless. From Wisconsin, from Michigan... the Potawatomi, the Ottawa, and the Chippewa of the Three Fires Confederacy were pushed into cars still soiled by cattle with little clean air, food, or water.

"Ogehmawahbee saw all of this happening and as he entered the cattle car, he renewed his promise to his daughter. He vowed to return home to his people. He would not die. And so... many were taken away.

"The journey by rails took many days. Ogehmawahbee always looked for the sun....just as he once had when he and others traveled west to make war on the Sioux. He knew that they were heading West and South. He remembered and counted the days. He counted the nights.

"The people were given very little to drink and only a handful of parched corn to eat. The terrible journey became blazing hot in the day from the sun... cold at night by the moon... wet when the rain came. Many of the people died along the way. But always Ogehmawahbee remembered his promise to return. This promise brought him strength.

"One morning, the train stopped. The doors opened. Fresh air rushed into the cars. The people, too weak and too ill to even move, were pulled and dragged from the cattle cars by the soldiers. Dumped onto the ground, their eyes at first blinded by the sunlight, they began to look around them. What was this strange land? Where were the maple trees to sweeten the springtime and to nourish? Where were the birch trees to build their canoes? Where were the black ash trees to make their baskets? Where were the cedar trees to construct bark homes? Where were the lakes to fish for food? Where were the forests in which to hunt? In Kansas, the people found none of these! Ogehmawahbee saw only rolling grass as far as the eye could see. How could one build shelter here from the unrelenting sun and the cold of the nights? Where would one find food to feed the people?

"Then the soldiers and the train left leaving the people alone in this place.

"Ogehmawahbee looked around. What a pitiful state the people were in. What kind of nation would do such a thing as this to any people? He could not understand it. But now was not the time to question. Now the people must survive. Those who were able found rocks and began to dig with their hands and with the rocks into the sides of sloping hills to make shelter. They searched for puddles and small ponds for water. They made traps and used rocks to kill small animals... even rodents. The people must eat to find strength. Many people died. Some survived. Many stories could be told of this place. Ogehmawahbee's story is just one story. But Ogehmawahbee survived and became strong, and this is his story.

"As the people's strength grew, they held council once more. Someone must return to rally those left behind. Someone must tell that many of the people had survived. Who could travel stealthily? Who could remember the way home? Must some stay to help others who were sure to come? Would it be best to travel alone or in a group? Could they get home before the time of snow and hunger? In the end, they chose Ogehmawahbee as one who should go. Those who tried to return would travel alone. All the others would remain in Kansas to care for the new arrivals, weak from the journey.

"Ogehmawahbee knew the time to keep his promise had come. He must travel east and north. Just as once the Chippewa had traveled East after they raided their enemy, the Sioux, he must reach the woodlands again before the winter snows came... the time that made travel hard... the time of cold.

"Ogehmawahbee also knew that once he left the people, that he could not trust anyone else. He could not trust the Indians of other Nations. He could not trust the whites. Because as soon as anyone sees one Indian running in the woods, someone would fire on him with bows and arrows. Some settler would shoot to kill. The only time that he could travel would be at night.

"But Ogehmawahbee's vision grew strong as he traveled by foot. The stars and the sun guided him. By night and day, if an enemy lurked, there would be a warning. Nobody could get nearer to him than just a certain distance. Sometimes he stole ponies.

"When he came to a river, he would swim across if he could. When the current proved too strong, he sought broken trees to make a raft. He didn't have anything to cut the logs with, you know, and those rafts do not float straight across a river. So he would have to follow the edges and avoid settlements on the rivers. Those rivers gave him a terrible time. And there are a lot of rivers to cross between here and Kansas.

"When he came to the great Mississippi, Ogehmawahbee turned north. In time, he entered the state that we now call Minnesota. He knew where he was! The fierce Sioux lived here. He had been here before. He respected these skilled warriors. Ogehmawahbee felt very thankful. Even if he needed to be very careful, he knew his way home from here. The woodlands would protect him and provide for him. Soon he found his way to Canada and to Manitoulin Island.

"What a celebration the people gave upon his return. Now the people knew that some of the people taken had also survived the terrible journey. Five long years had passed since Ogehmawahbee began his incredible journey. Much had changed since he had been kidnapped. Smallpox and disease had killed many of the Chippewa who had not been relocated and who had remained. Settlers had taken away much of the land. On Manitoulin, the Spirit Island, his wife and daughter had waited and had survived to welcome him home.

"But Ogehmawahbee never forgot those he left behind in Kansas. Out of respect, he did not boast about his incredible journey."

Grandfather Michael-John paused again for a long moment looking into the children's faces. "You know little ones... we don't know much about why the incredible journey took so long...for once our people could run great distances on well known trails in a period of days and weeks, not years to cross this great land. Even when the soldiers took Ogehmawahbee away once more, this time to Oklahoma, he returned home to the Chippewa and the Great Lakes. Ogehmawahbee would not leave his family nor give up his home in the Great Lakes.

"The Chippewa followed his spirit returning to the Islands of Mackinac and Les Cheneaux. We are still here today.

"So I will say, Chum na gee zha gut... it is a good day."

Thus Michael-John ended his story around the fire in the light of the Munido Gieezis moon, the Great Spirit Moon. A story to be told again around new fires... a story to warm the ears and hearts... a story often told of Ogehmawahbee and his incredible journey. A story of just one of the people who survived relocation. Ahow.

Appendix

In his written records, Mike Osogwin Sr. spelled "Ogehmawahbee" as follows: Way-ge-maw-waw-be. The text uses Ogehmawahbee because this was the way Mike Osogwin Jr. remembered his father and uncle saying the name in the oral tradition. Details omitted from the tape and used in the story text come from collective memory of Mike Osogwin Jr. and Oliver Birge or the research of Moira Z. Wilson and Yvonne Peer.

Mike Osogwin Sr. (1892-1974) [son of Joseph Osogwin and Teresa Beaver] married Catherine Mary Agnes Blackbird (1905-1990) [daughter of Clement Blackbird (AKA Truman Blackbird) and Christine Animikiw (Aleek)].

Mike Osogwin Sr. and his brother, John Osogwin, were friends of Oliver Birge. These two men and Peter John Beaver were three men that Oliver Birge knew from his early childhood throughout his adult life. Mr. Birge held these men in great esteem.

Mike Osogwin Jr. carries a sacred pipe for the Chippewa and is known by the name, Moy-Say-Ghe-Sis (First Light of Day) and his wife Marianne or Wah-Shkwa-Mee-Guin-A-Quay (White Feather Woman) who has Cherokee ancestry reside near Hessel, Michigan.

Moira Wilson and Yvonne Peer attended Lake Superior State University as returning students. Their mutual interests led them to co-present a paper at the 1993 Native American Studies Conference. Yvonne Hogue-Peer currently is a pro-tem curator for the soon to be realized Fort Brady Military Museum to be located at Lake Superior State University as well as doing research for Great Lakes genealogy through Genequest.

Brian F. Wilson, son of Moira and Paul Wilson, works as a Medical Illustrator for Medical Legal Art of Atlanta. Brian resides in Marietta, Georgia with his wife Kelly.

Reprinted with the permission of Yvonne-Hogue Peer, of Sault Ste. Marie, MI. 49783 and Susan M. Schacher, Ed., <u>Celebration of Indigenous Thought and Expression</u>, "Oral Tradition and Print: The Stories of Mike and John Osogwin", Moira Z. Dibert Wilson and Yvonne Peer, p. 163-172.
Sault Ste. Marie, MI: Lake Superior State University Press. 1996

Oral Tradition and Print:
The Stories of John Osogwin and Mike Osogwin

Moira Z. Dibert Wilson and Yvonne Peer
Lake Superior State University

As Heinrich Schliemann once found Troy by reading the Iliad, so may today's students and historians re-investigate our past by listening to the stories from the Native American oral traditions. These stories dramatically focus on human events that must not be dusty footnotes in history texts. During the Christmas season in 1955, John Osogwin permitted Dick Church to record his words. Thirteen years later, in 1968, Mike Osogwin permitted his words to be recorded by Oliver Birge of Hessel, Michigan. Oliver Birge kept copies of these two tapes which provide the substance of this paper.

The stories printed here renew the hope that they will be told aloud again as they should be in keeping with the oral tradition. Modifying the format used by Dennis Tedlock in <u>Finding the Center</u>, the poetical nature of these tales will be readily apparent. To read these stories aloud, the instructions are quite simple. They are as follows: (1) [...] means pause at least half a second each time before the new line begins, and [*] means a pause of at least two seconds; (2) use a soft voice for words in small type, and a loud one for words in capitals; still louder for larger letters; (3) crescendo or soften words if capitals or small type letters take place within a word; (4) [-] between words in a line means say each word distinctly and clearly in a soft measured rhythm; (5) ^ means a rising inflection then drop at the end of the word; and lastly (6) tones of voice or other staging directions are indicated by italics. Complete original transcripts will be available in 1995 or 1996.

In this paper rare minor deletions and rare line order changes have been made to adhere to space requirements.

So let the wordarrows fly as one begins with John Osogwin's tale. Wordarrows is a word coined by Gerald Vizenor.

Dick Church asked: Who was this a ... This fella you were telling me about one time that when he laid down the mosquitoes wouldn't get on him... The guy that was kidnapped?

John Osogwin: Oh, yes, oh that was my grandfather ... That is my mother's grandfather ... Yes that was ... Nickodemous Shedawin Osogwin. Now there isn't any more Shedawins ceptin ... Now you know this fella ... Que qui wick (phonetic spelling, may not be accurate].

Dick Church: You mean Charlie Shedawin?

John Osogwin: Yeah, that's the only Shedawin that's left. That was A Shedawin who raised my mother. That was ... that was a my mother's grandfather ... He lived in Beaver Island, they lived in Beaver Island and in the summer time ... They lived in ... Aaaa Black River I think they called it. Just the other side of Epoufette ... The old grand, grandfather took my mother, an most the summer, they lived in Beaver Island, that is the fall and spring they lived in Black River ... But when she was big enough, she used tah watch the old man never does anything, lay around an, an could be laying anywheres, and ... by God ... The mosquitoes never bit him ... (chuckle)*

You know at one time during the treaties ... There was a treaty at a ... At a Detroit ... and Chicago, ... And afterwhile kept coming further north ... See the northern Indians couldn't go to Detroit. It'd tak'em all summer ... They hadn't ... Much idea when the treaty Boat WOULD COme ... Well they took away a couple bunches of Indians out of Beaver Island ... And he was one of them... And aaaah ... I never did know where they took him to (sounds gently puzzled)*

Well my great grandfather said that they took'm as far as the railroad went ... At that time ... And they dumped them in the prairie ... And both times ... He (trails off)*

The first ... The-first time he was taken ... To KANsas ... He was gone SIX years ... But he came ^BAAaaack ... He said he had to travel most of the time ... (^inflect voice up, almost like a question, drop at end of word) At ^night ... He couldn't trust anybody ... He - couldn't - trust - the - whites*

Or he couldn't - trust - the - Indians*

'Cause as soon as you see one Indian running in the wood someplaces'll ... Fire at them ... With their bows and arrows ... And the settlers would shoot, would shoot an kill'm ... The only time that he could travel WAS AT ^NIGHT ... And there'd be places where he could ... Steal the ponies ... Well then he had ... He knew the direction where his home is ... You see, it is over there ... See ... But he go'd there he run into a river ... Well some places he have tah ... Cut a log ... And if he didn't have anything to cut it with ... He would manage to go pick up some broken trees and he'd make a raft ... And he'd go across this river ... And from there to Kansas there is quite - a - few - rivers - to come -across*

Well it took him a long time and he had to do this work at night ... And it didn't make any difference where he was at night or at in the daytime ... If there was any enemy there'd be a warning ... Because ... Nobody could of course get nearer to him than just ascertain distance ... That is, he'd duck out of there But now after he learned, the second time that he was taken He had a longer distance to go ... But he ... He had already ^LEArned ... Sometimes he knew he'd follow this river ... On the edge ... And sometimes he couldn't do that ... Because there would be Indians settling, or a livin on ... The river banks ... He had a terrible time ... (John chuckled softly, there is a tone of irony in the laughter)

Dick Church: (Dick's question -is strongly stated) But <u>why</u> did they take him away in the first place?

John Osogwin: Oh we'll, they wanna GET RID OF the Indians that's all. They came in there with a two, sometimes three vessels ... With all kinds of blankets, and all kinds of kitchen utensils, pots and pans and knives,to give it to the Indians, this is the treaty time, and then they had... Some sweet stuff ... And after while ... They came with the ah... Cheap jewelry ... Well-aaah you take ... Cheap jewelry will attract a lot of poor people ... And then of course each is the same way ... And it mixes the same way ... Oftener they came and saw the Indians over the years, they had ... To ^LEArn ... What would attract all of them intah the boat ... It would be a ... JEWELry in some places, and in some places it would be...And in some places would be, would be - drinks ... Well they a...They a set the tables ... It was pert' near the end of their ... Their aaahh journey to go back, they were going to give the Indians a farewell ...a treat. And they set the aaahh ... The eats ...Down in ... Down in the hull. Now, you know how it is ... Boats?*

And they had those here hatches ... All'm with hinges on the one side ... An then they catch on the other side ... And then all you haf'ta do is ... And when she slams

She's locked ... Well they had this here eats ...An the ...And the drinks .. And the jewelry ...An all ... All down in ... An SOME of them wouldn't go down ...But they coaxed everybody down in there ... And when they got all ... all - of - them ... And some they wouldn't go ... They put them in the LAKE ... (both men laugh)

Dick Church: (Again the question strongly stated) Well, who did that, the fur traders or the government?

John Osogwin: THE GOVERNMENT * And they said when we got to Chicago ... Where ever these here vessels landed ...We were right near the railroad ... Parked cars ... Pushed us in there, see they had ... They were empty handed... They couldn't fight and they couldn't do - nothin' ... And he said All little kids ... Some of them ... Very few kids ... Cause the ... The kids were left home ... Some of 'em were from Wisconsin, some in the different parts of Michigan ... An during this treaty time,- there'd be just ... One - or two people in one family would go to the treaty and bring back their ... What ever they were given to*

Anyways [he] she was just a young man then ... He couldn't fight...He couldn't do nothin. So he said, when we got...In ah, ah to the train stop ... Open the doors ... Shoved us all out... We had nothing to eat ... And we had nothin in water ... An we had nothin at'tall ... Just empty handed. (voice drops. following spoken very softly) There ... there's where they were. So they survived, lived and just as though they didn't know their own luck.

Dick Church: (Dick's statement is said slowly, almost incredulously) You don't read about that in the history books though. They don't tell you nothin' about that.

John Osogwin: Oh no no, that would be a disgrace to a wise (hint of a chuckle)... A nation.

(Both men laugh.)

Thirteen years later Mike Osogwin would re-tell this tale and give additional information. Understatement hallmarks these tales of survival as well.

Mike Osogwin: They usedtah to take the Indians out west... And all that, from Beaver Island, away out, you know and ah... From Beaver Island youknow, they sent them out youknow and let them out where the railroad ended youknow and ah, they sent um out twice, I know. First time they sent em out where the rail road ended, youknow, that's where they sent them out, then of course ... He was just a young buck, he was already married though but he made the trip youknow. He managed all right to get back youknow.

As he was saying youknow, that a long time gettin over des rivers youknow

He hadtah make a raft sometimes ... Some of the-rivers youknow what he was just a young feller, he'd get a log ... Get on top of it and he start paddle across (chuckle) but it would be startin' here youknow, it wouldn't be straight across, that ... Current you know would carry him a long ways, so then the ... Then the last time he went down to the Oklahoma Chippewa, some were in Kansas and Ioway, youknow, and also in ah ... in ah Oklahoma, where some there were of these Indians from Beaver Island ... Yah, but they didn't do it at Mackinac, you know

But so they ... Both times, they, youknow, should have tumbled the second time, youknow ... youknow ... That's kinda of a queer youknow, they didn't... But, to take a bit the second time, youknow, Of course they were (spoken in a slight rush) Like when they were gettin' every thing youknow, gettin' a treaty youknow, gettin' a payment youknow, and everything an ... (resume normal cadence) And finally they had everything down in the bottom of those old vessels you know ... And, take'em down there, and show them all this ... It. was all right, and finally they give'em this ... This banquet youknow. The banquet youknow, well ... Some ... Went down dah to eat ... and some DIDN'T, you know they were a little bit leeeaaary ... About... Down there ... Why didn't they have it on the

deck? youknow... And they up and peer'd down in the bottom. So at that time, that... that ... Whatever wouldn't go in... Could throw them over board, they either drowned you know... Figure that's quite a ways, I know how far the rest aways ... The handcuffs are ...
... And if you didn't make it ashore, it was alright to the ... To those who ever were doing, the paymasters' job, you know ... And of course, an all the Indians could swim anyways so it didn't make any difference ... They all managed to get ashore and then they ... and here's - all - those - husbands ... and maybe - the young mothers are - gone, ... and - the daughters, - and the - young - families -
they left an, at Beaver Island ... An still Beaver Island came up again all right but all the ... Old folks were gone. Both times**

Oliver: Well, Mike, where did they give'em the small pox or black plague?

Osogwin: They give'em at Mackinac Island.

Oliver: Mackinac.

Osogwin: That's after they set these things in there ... In 1820 ... In the 1820 treaty is the time that THOSE BLANKETS was issued!

* (Begin quietly) And of course, there were just thousands, we don't know how many died this way, youknow.* And ... Many of them went west. Youknow. As I was saying .- My great grandfather ... he'ah picked up all the babies youknow * Got children that he knows that there was something wrong ... He had to go through, he came as far as St. Ignace youknow, round an up, what ever he could make in a day ... You know. Followed the shoreline, and he picked up whatever he can carry, and h'carry them home ... Cause - he -couldn't* (a deep breath) * He couldn't - let - the babies - die -there - an all ... See'a their folk's was all ^dead ... And they was just all scabs youknow ... Youknow that they had some of'a kinda scab

... ... So that they really know'd there was something given to them ... Yah the Indians all the time, and some of the old folks still BLAMED that ... The missionary ... An ... so ... for a long time ... We didn't, youknow I ... heard it from my mother, and then after that youknow, that there were ... Was this terrible thing, youknow, all these Indians .. 0 um hum. and ... Dying - you - know. (trails off)

An irony may be found in the final words of the John Osogwin tape. "You know at first I didn't believe the Indian History ... a lot of things, but now .... as

I grew older, I've commenced to think back, my mother and father would sit..." there the tape ended. Thirty-eight years later, Mike Osogwin Jr. would say when asked about his father and his uncle "I grew up hearing those stories, and I didn't believe them until I was working in California. One of the men who worked for me from Oklahoma told me about the Chippewas in Oklahoma that keep to themselves."

The Osogwins represent centuries of oral tradition. Their narratives are unique, yet parallel narratives of other Indians who have spoken of events which occurred within their lifetimes or the lifetimes of their elders.

The Europeans, who have relied upon written tradition for centuries, have recorded their activities among the Indians. We are dependent upon those written records, which may or may not be accurate, because of the differences in perspective. We are able to trace these events only as accurately as they were recorded in those written records. The Americans enumerated the Indians, including the Osogwins and the Shedawins. These enumerations are to be found locally on the Durant Rolls and the annuity payment lists, both of which include the Osogwin and Shedawin families (U.S. Annuities, 1870; Durant Roll, 1907).

Once the treaty negotiations began the Indians lived in constant fear of removal. Removal policies were a preferred means of clearing the Indians from lands desired by the pioneers and were suggested as early as 1803 by Thomas Jefferson. In 1820, President-Andrew Jackson said that it was "high time to do away with the farce of treating with the Indian tribes" and added that the only reason the Indians remained was due to the "generosity" of the United States Government. Secretary of War John C. Calhoun, echoed the sentiments of Jackson when he also suggested removal policies (Dunbar, 1980). Even Indian agents, like Thomas McKenney, who had advocated assimilation prior to his tour of the Indians in 1827, upon returning reversed his policies and favored Indian removal (Dunbar,. 1980). He felt, it seems, that the Indians were not adjusting to his assimilation policies and were continuing to act out their roles as Indians. Politicians were strongly in favor of removal to protect the Indians from "debauchery" (Gilbert,'1984).

Removal policies became official in 1830 with the Removal Act (Dunbar, 1980). As each new treaty was signed, the Indians came closer to the fact of removal. Some Indians feared removal so much that they removed themselves (McClurken, 1991). Others, like the Potowatami, were hunted down and forcibly removed (Gilbert, 1984). Occasionally, non-Indians would give money or assistance to the Indians, but in most cases, were not interested in their welfare-they simply wanted the Indians' land (Dunbar, 1980). The British gave gifts to Indians who were residents of Canada, so many went to Manitoulin Island and other areas of lower Canada (McClurken, 1991). Some headed west. Many hid out and later returned to their Michigan homeland. Others never returned (Bauman, 1952).

The Beaver Island Indians were slated for removal following the signing of the 1836 Treaty of Washington (Article I., fourth paragraph, Magnaghi, 1984). Between the years of 1820 and 1830 the non-Indian population of Michigan had grown from 8,765 to 31,640. During the next four years it tripled and by 1840 had swollen to well over 200,000 people (Bald, 1954). When Frederic Baraga visited Beaver Island in 1831 there were only Indians living there (Verwyst, 1900). When James Strang investigated the islands in 1846-47, all he found on the main island were a few Irish fisherman (Williams, 1905).

Removal was not the only effective means of controlling the Indian population. Extermination had also come into use. At Fort Pitt, British Commander-in-Chief Sir Jeffrey Amherst suggested "sending smallpox" among the Indians (Parkman, 1870), Father Gabriel Richard was suspect among the Indians because he and a smallpox epidemic both arrived at L'Arbre Croche in 1799 (Magnaghi, 1984). Many diseases were innocently carried to the Indians, but others were purposely sent.

Osogwin (because of the oral history tradition, one Osogwin speaks for all Osogwins) alludes to the 1820 Treaty as the time of extermination attempts, but the 1836 Treaty seems more likely. Thousands of Indians received annuity payments at Mackinac in 1837, and thousands of Indians died in a smallpox epidemic that same year (Tanner, 1987). "Two Chippewa chiefs told Major John Garland that American Fur Company traders in secret council told the Indians that the goods given in place of specie were infected with disease and obviously evidence of the government's bad faith toward the Indians." They further stated that next year only goods would be distributed (Magnaghi, 1984). The smallpox epidemic of 1837 "decimated entire villages" while survivors fled in fear to Canada and other areas (Emmert, 1952). Henry Schoolcraft reported that the Saginaw Band lost a third or more of its population to smallpox in the 1837 epidemic (Emmert, 1952).

Other narratives told of similar circumstances. Andrew Blackbird's book, History of the Ottawa and Chippewa Indians of Michigan told of officials who sent "mouldy particles" enclosed within nested, tin boxes. The Crooked Tree, a book published in Harbor Springs, contains a similar narrative, but the boxes are silver and contain smallpox contaminated "trinkets" to be distributed by the chiefs to the people of their villages. Osogwin speaks of smallpox-infected blankets. Whatever vehicle was used for distribution, the results were equally disastrous.

In response to the the Indians' protests about being removed, the government contracted with private "conductors" to physically remove the Indians by boat or rail, and this is corroborated by the Osogwin narratives (Cleland, 1975). Removal was not as effective as extermination, but by the 1840s most of the Indians were gone from Michigan (Dunbar, 1980). When the removal policy was discontinued, it was because there were not enough Indians left in Michigan to pose any problems to the government. By 1855 the Allotment Act had already taken effect, although it was not yet official, and the remaining Indians were supposedly given small parcels of and (Wright, 1917). This left the remaining lands to be sold to the non-Indians. Although Beaver Island was to have had a reservation for the Indians, the only islands still held by the Indians were High and Garden Islands (Tanner, 1987).

Few, if any, Michigan officials were working toward assisting the Indians. Governor Cass was suspected of having financial interests in the American Fur Company (Dunbar, 1980). Indian Agent Henry R. Schoolcraft was accused by the Indians of showing favoritism in the distribution of annuities and supplies because he had Indian relatives (Magnaghi, 1984). He was also suspect in a number of land schemes (Dunbar, 1980). These agents served their personal interests better than those of the Indians.

When the French occupied the area, it was not uncommon for a "foreign exchange policy" to take place in which the French would ship bright young males over to America to learn the Indian languages and cultures. This policy also worked in reverse as promising young Indian males were sent to France for the same purpose. This seems to have been the case for the elder Osogwin.

Osogwin mentions the name Shedawin a few times and the 1907 Durant Roll also lists the Shedawins as relatives. Joe Sr. was married to an Indian woman named Theresa whose family name translates to Shedawin and she originated from the Traverse Band. Joseph Osogwin would have been born in or about 1849, which would have brought him onto the scene at a time when the Indians' world was under siege. Without the oral history tradition and the receptive audience for this lore, the story of this period would not now be available. Andrew Blackbird, a noted Indian author and scholar, speaks eloquently of his father, who held the position of speaker for the council of the Ottawa and Chippewa in the Traverse area. The elder Blackbird passed the mantle on to Osogwin, who spent his life in that role, before passing it on to his son, thus beginning a hallowed Osogwin family tradition (Blackbird, 1887). The presentation today continues that tradition. The Osogwins had been "waiting" for someone when Moira Wilson called for an interview.

They felt that it would only be a matter of time until their narratives would become important to an audience other than to their own young people. The narratives were honest, accurate, and we sincerely hope, interesting

Acknowledgements:

We are deeply indebted to Richard Church and Oliver Birge who with great foresight made the recordings of the Osogwin brothers, John and Mike. Most particularly to Oliver Birge, who valued the tapes and shared them with the authors.

We also wish to acknowledge Mike Osogwin Jr. and his wife, Marianne Osogwin, who welcomed our questions and rejoiced at the prospect for the oral tradition to continue for future generations.

References

Bald, F C. (1954). Michigan in four centuries New York: Harper & Brothers.
Bauman, R. F. (1952). Kansas, Canada, or starvation. Michigan History. Lansing: Michigan Historical Commission.
Blackbird, A. J. (1887). History of the Ottawa and Chippewa Indians of Michigan. Ypsilanti, Michigan: The Ypsilanti Job Printing House. Reprint; Little Traverse Regional Historical Society, Inc.
Cleland, C. E. (1975). A brief history of Michigan Indians. Lansing: Michigan Department of State.
Dunbar, W. F. (1965). Michigan: a history of the wolverine state. Grand Rapids: William B. Eerdman's.
Dunbar, W. F. (1980). Michigan: a history of the wolverine state. Grand Rapids:Revised Edition; George S. May, William Eerdman's.
Gilbert, H. F. (1984). Tonquish tales. Plymouth, Michigan: Pilgrim Heritage Press.
Magnaghi, R. M. (1984). A guide to the Indians of Michigan's Upper Peninsula: 1621-1900. Marquette: Belle Fontaine Press.
McClurken, J. M. (1991). Gab-Baeh-Jhagwah-Buk, The way it happened. East Lansing: Michigan State University Museum.
Parkman, F. (1991). The conspiracy of Pontiac. New York: Literary Classics of the United States.
Tanner, H. H. (Ed.). (1987). Atlas of Great Lakes Indian history,' Norman: University of Oklahoma Press.
Tedlock, D. (1972). Finding the center; Narrative poetry of the Zuni Indians. New York: Dial Press
United States Government (1870). Annuity payrolls of Ottawa and Chippewa Indians of Michigan. Ann Arbor: University Microfilms International.
United States Government (1907). Durant roll. Ann Arbor: University Microfilms International.
Verwyst, P. C., O.F.M. (1905). Life and labors of Right Reverend Frederic Bagaga. Milwaukee, Wisconsin: M. H. Wiltzuis.
Wright, 1. C. (1917). The crooked tree. Binghamton: Vail-Ballou.

John Osogwin
(pictured right)
Photo courtesy of Les Cheneaux Historical Association

Mike Osogwin, Sr., Catherine Osogwin, and Family
(pictured below)
Photo courtesy of Les Cheneaux Historical Association

Mike Osogwin, Jr.
(pictured left at the "Gathering of Eagles",
Pow-wow, Hessel, Michigan)
Photo courtesy of Jerry Causley

Marianne Osogwin
(pictured below)
Photo courtesy of Kate Rudolph

Moira Z. Wilson
(pictured left)
Photo courtesy of Wilsons

Brian F. Wilson
(pictured right)
Photo courtesy of Wilsons